BIBLE 20
THE STORY OF ...

CONTENTS

Author: **Iva Grant**
Editor-in-Chief: Richard W. Wheeler, M.A.Ed.
Editor: Betty B. Moore, M.A.
Consulting Editor: W. Mel Alexander, Th.M.,Ph.D
Revision Editor: Alan Christopherson, M.S.

Alpha Omega Publications

300 North McKemy Avenue, Chandler, Arizona 85226-2618

ALPHA OMEGA
PUBLICATIONS

Learn with the Bridgestone characters:

When you see me, I will help your teacher explain the exciting things you are expected to do.

When you do actions with me, you will learn how to write, draw, match words, read, and much more.

You and I will learn about matching words, listening, drawing, and other fun things in your lessons.

Follow me and I will show you new, exciting truths, that will help you learn and understand what you study. Let's learn!

THE STORY OF JOSEPH

Hello _____ .

Print your name.

    In this LIFEPAC you will meet Joseph. He will tell you about his family and how he lived. Joseph will tell you about the animals. Joseph will tell you about his home. Joseph's father will tell stories. You will find out how Joseph learned and worked and played. You will see how Joseph worshiped God.

    You will learn that God takes care of us because He loves us.

Objectives

Read these objectives. They tell you what you will be able to do when you have finished this LIFEPAC.

1. You will be able to tell someone about Joseph's home.
2. You will be able to name the way Joseph worshiped God.
3. You will be able to tell someone how he can be saved by Jesus.
4. You will be able to tell how God can make a good thing come out of the bad thing someone did.

NEW WORDS

altar (al tar). A special place used to worship God.

beans. A kind of a food.

bow. To bend your body in a very polite way.

camel (cam el). A large animal with a long neck and a hump
  on its back.

circle (cir cle). A ring. Something round with a hole in the
  middle.

curtain (cur tain). A hanging cloth to close part of the tent.

donkey (don key). An animal like a horse, but smaller.

famine (fam ine). A time when there is no food to eat.

flour. What is made by wheat or other grain by grinding it.

grain. Seeds from plants.

grind. Crush something into very small pieces by pushing and
  turning a stone on it.

heavenly Father (heav en ly fa ther). God.

hook. A piece of wood to hang things on.

lesson (les son). Something to learn.

mill. Two flat stones used to grind seeds between.

oil lamp. A small dish to hold oil. The oil was set on fire to
  make light.

oxen (ox en). Cattle that work.

pole. A tall piece of wood.

pour. Put something like water or milk in a cup.

pray (pray). Talk to God.

prison (pri son). A place where people who break the law are locked up.

ruler (ruler). Like a king.

saddle (sad dle). A seat for a rider on an animal.

secret (se cret). Something you do not tell anyone.

sin. To disobey God.

slave. A man or a woman who is owned by someone else.

stylus (sty lus). A small, sharp stick to write on with wet clay.

tablet (tab let). Something to write on.

thin. One side is very close to the other side.

thorny (thor ny). Small things on a bush that are sharp.

trader (trad er). Someone who buys and sells things.

wise. To know much about something.

women (wo men). More than one woman.

worship (wor ship). Pray to God and praise Him.

These words will appear in **boldface** (darker print) the first time they are used.

I. JOSEPH AS A BOY

Hello! My name is Bill. I want to tell you about a dream I had about Joseph. I was reading about Joseph in my Bible in the book of Genesis just before I fell asleep. I dreamed that I visited Joseph in Bible times.

Joseph lived far away. Joseph lived long ago.

In my dream, I came to a strange land. I saw many tents. I was in Bible lands! A boy was nearby. I talked to him. It was Joseph! He told me all about his work and family. He told me about his work and how he **worshiped** God. I had fun. Let me tell you the story as it happened in my dream.

WORDS TO STUDY

altar	(al tar)	A special place used to worship God.
beans		A kind of a food.
camel	(cam el)	A large animal with a long neck and a hump on its back.
circle	(cir cle)	A ring. Something round with a hole in the middle.
curtain	(cur tain)	A hanging cloth to close part of the tent.
donkey	(don key)	An animal like a horse, but smaller.
flour		What is made by wheat or other grain by grinding it.
grain		Seeds from plants.
grind		Crush something into very small pieces by pushing and turning a stone on it.
hook		A piece of wood to hang things on.
lesson	(les son)	Something to learn.
mill		Two flat stones used to grind seeds between.

oil lamp		A small dish to hold oil. The oil was set on fire to make light.
oxen	(ox en)	Cattle that work.
pole		A tall piece of wood.
pour		Put something like water or milk in a cup.
pray		Talk to God.
saddle	(sad dle)	A seat for a rider on an animal.
sin		To disobey God.
stylus	(sty lus)	A small, sharp stick to write on with wet clay.
tablet	(tab let)	Something to write on.
thorny	(thor ny)	Small things on a bush that are sharp.
women	(wo men)	More than one woman.
worship	(wor ship)	Pray to God and praise Him.

Special Words

Benjamin   Joseph

Jacob   Reuben

Ask your teacher to say these words with you.

Teacher Check _____

Initial   Date

page 5 (five)

HOME LIFE

"Hello, I'm Bill. Are you Joseph?"

"Yes, my name is Joseph."

"I was reading about you in my Bible. I wondered what it was like to live in Bible times. I fell asleep and here I am!"

"I am glad you came to visit me. Come with me, Bill. I want you to meet my family. I have ten big brothers and one little brother. I also have one sister."

 Write the word that belongs in the sentence.

1.1   Bill dreamed that he lived in _____ times.

1.2   Bill dreamed that he visited _____ .

1.3   Joseph had _____ big brother(s).

1.4   Joseph had _____ little brother(s).

"That is the biggest circle of tents I have ever seen. Do the animals always stay in the circle?"

"Oh yes, these animals stay in the circle because they are safe from the wild animals here. We take our sheep other places to eat grass."

"You have some **camels**, too. I have seen camels before."

"We put big, long bags on our camels when we move. We put our tents and other things in the bags. The camels are strong. They can carry heavy bags. We drink the camel's milk, too. The camel's milk is very good."

"We also have **donkeys**. Donkeys can carry baskets of bread or fruit. Sometimes my father ties a box on the donkey's back. My father lets me ride in the box. Would you like to ride in a donkey box?"

"Yes, I would. Do you have any other animals?"

"We have cows that give us milk and meat. We have **oxen** to work in our fields. Come with me and I will show you my home."

Work this puzzle.

1.5   Look for these animal names in the puzzle. When you find the animal name, put a circle around it. The first one is done for you.

ANIMALS   COW   GOAT   SHEEP

CAMEL   DONKEY   OXEN

R	S	Q	P	M	N	O	C	A	B	L	Y
D	B	S	Z	V	L	M	O	D	R	S	D
T	U	H	X	N	B	A	W	R	D	W	O
Z	O	E	P	Q	V	Y	D	L	M	D	N
H	E	E	U	S	R	O	N	P	K	L	K
C	A	P	H	D	O	X	E	N	G	S	E
B	R	N	U	S	D	F	G	R	O	Z	Y
C	A	M	E	L	I	L	A	P	A	U	X
L	C	D	P	H	R	Z	D	M	T	O	B
T	V	Z	L	O	A	N	I	M	A	L	S

"My home is a tent. We put our tents in a circle. We put our tents where there is grass for our animals to eat. When we need more grass, we move our tents to a new place."

"Does all your family live here?"

"Yes, my older brothers live in these tents. My oldest brother, Reuben, lives in that tent. Benjamin is my younger brother. He lives with me in that tent."

"We make our tents out of goat hair. Each tent has two or three rooms. One room in the tent is for men. One room is for **women** and sometimes we use one room in the tent for animals."

"I like to live in a tent. Back home, we live in tents when we go to the mountains."

"Come inside the tent and look around," said Joseph. "We put **hooks** on the tent **poles**. We hang baskets and clothes on the hooks. My father hangs his **saddles** on them."

"We have **curtains** that hang between the poles. These curtains make our rooms. We have curtains on the sides of the tents, too. We put the curtains on the sides of the tent down when it is cold," said Joseph.

"You have nice rugs on the ground. Where do you sleep?"

"Do you see those mats over there? We put those mats down on the ground. We lie down and use our coats to keep warm."

"When we go to the mountains, we sleep on something like that. We call them sleeping bags."

 Follow the numbers to finish the drawing.

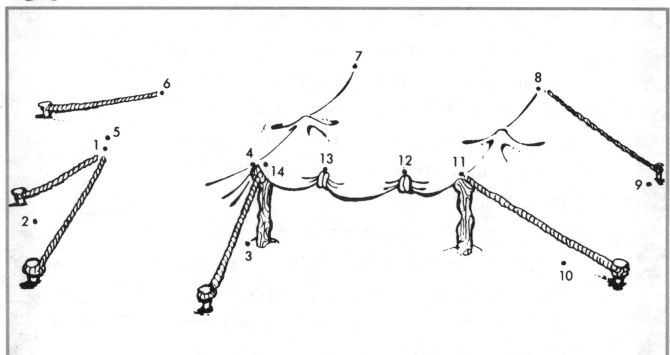

 Write the word in the blank.

1.6   Joseph lived in a large _____.

1.7   Joseph slept with his younger _____.

Find the word that best ends the sentence.

Each of the words follow this rule.

When **g** is followed by the letters **i**, **e**, or **y**, **g** has the soft sound of **j** as in **giant**. The letter **g** also has the hard sound as in the word **go**.

Write the word that best finishes the sentence.
You may want a helper to read the words with you.

1.8   Goliath was a _____ .

1.9   _____ juice is good to drink.

1.10   Jesus was laid in a _____ .

1.11   We play ball in the _____ .

1.12   An elephant is a _____ animal.

1.13   God loved us so much He _____ us His only Son.

manger
gave
giant
orange
gym
huge

Write the word from the box that has the hard /g/ sound.

1.14   _____

"See the bags around the tent poles. **Grain** is in the bags. We **grind** the grain in the **mill**. The women use the grain to make bread. We will eat some bread after a while."

"Where do you get your water?"

"Over there is a well. The well has a big stone cover on it. The cover keeps the water clean. Soon the men will take the cover off. The animals will get a drink."

This visit was exciting. I was tired. I sat on the ground to rest.

Joseph rested, too. We rested and watched the women. The women were getting food ready. The women used **thorny** sticks for a fire. Then the women put a pot of **beans** over the fire to cook.

Next, the women made bread. They put the grain on a stone and crushed it to make **flour**. Then they put milk and water in the flour and mixed it with their hands. They patted it out and baked it on hot stones.

The women put milk in animal skins. They shook the milk in the animal skins to make butter.

Color the picture of Joseph's family making butter.

Soon it was time to eat. Joseph and I washed our hands with water. Joseph **poured** some water over my hands. The men would eat first. Then the women and children would eat.

When it was time for the women and children to eat, we sat around a mat on the ground. The bowl of beans was in the middle. Everyone **prayed** to God before they ate. Then we dipped our bread in the bowl of beans and ate. We had goat's milk to drink, too.

"Do you ever have meat to eat?"

"Yes, we do. We have sheep, goat, and cow meat."

"Eating with our fingers is fun. At home we use forks, spoons and knives."

"Are you through eating? When we finish eating we will say a thank-you prayer to God. Then we will wash our hands."

The meal was very good.

 Write the answer in the blank. Then "track" your answer. The first one is done for you.

The fire was made with <u>thorny</u> bushes.

a l q (t) m c x (h) p d a (o) z b s (r) b x l (n) q s i (y)

1.15   The women made grain into _____ .

r z n d p f i g d e n l p n o m a c u p z r n d o

1.16   Milk was shaken in an animal skin to make _____ .

b l n u s q p d t d z x y w t m o e n o r p

1.17   We sat on the _____ around a mat "table" to eat.

w d e g h z i s r k a c o u m t e n r a x d

1.18   Joseph's family _____ before and after they ate.

q p z n o r k c u a m t z y p x e o m d u t m

1.19   We had _____ to drink.

r o s n m p z q s i t e x r l d b o k m n d

When it was dark outside, one of the women lit oil lamps. All of the family sat around their father, Jacob. He told them many stories.

Ask your teacher to help you learn the song "Give Me Oil in My Lamp."

Jacob talked about how God wants us to obey Him. Jacob told how God took care of Noah because Noah was good and obeyed God. He told about the big boat Noah had made and about all the animals that went in the boat.

Joseph liked the story about the Flood. Most of all he liked the part about the rainbow. The rainbow made Joseph think about God. Joseph looked over at me and smiled.

I whispered, "I have seen a rainbow."

"I like rainbows. The rainbow makes me think about God."

Everyone loved the stories and wanted to listen to more, but it was time for bed. The girls rolled out the mats while we blew out the lamps. All of us lay down on the mats and put our coats over us to keep warm.

I lay in bed thinking for a long time. Everything was so different!

I could see the night sky. I could see a lot of things around the tent. The other

tents were out there. The animals were
asleep nearby. Everyone in the tent was
asleep. Joseph was my friend. I thought
about tomorrow. What would we do?
What would we see?

 Circle the best answer.

1.20   Pick a good name for this part of the story.
      a. Lighting the Lamp.
      b. Time for Bed.
      c. Jacob's Stories.

1.21   What will I do next?
      a. go back home
      b. find out what Joseph does all day
      c. go for a walk

 **Find a word on a star that belongs in the
sentence. Write the word on the blank.** Remember
that in words like night the i is long and the gh is
silent.

1.22   When it is day _____ , we will get up.

1.23   Joseph lived near a _____ mountain.

1.24   Joseph tried to do what God said was

        _____ .

1.25   The sky was a pretty _____ .

WORK

"Good morning," called Joseph. "It is time to get up. We will have some bread and milk for breakfast. I want you to spend the day with me. We will do the things I do every day."

"I want to visit your school."

"We do not have school. My father and older brothers teach me."

We ate our food and got ready to leave. Joseph put his coat on. The coat had many colors in it.

"What a colorful coat!"

"My father gave it to me. Almost everybody likes my coat. Are you ready to go, Bill?"

As we walked away from the tent, we could see Joseph's brothers looking at us. They did not seem very friendly.

All the brothers knew that Jacob loved them. They knew that Jacob loved Joseph the most. Jacob gave Joseph the beautiful coat. Joseph's brothers were not very happy about that.

Color these coats.

1.26

| Color this coat yellow. | Color this coat red and yellow. | Color this coat many colors. |

a **pretty** coat   a **prettier** coat   the **prettiest** coat

Make more new words. Change the y to i and add -er and -est. The first one is done for you.

	-er (more)	**-est** (most)
pretty	prettier	prettiest
1.27 merry	_____	_____
1.28 dirty	_____	_____
1.29 early	_____	_____
1.30 heavy	_____	_____
1.31 hungry	_____	_____

Joseph and I went to his father, Jacob, first. Jacob gave him a writing **lesson**.

I watched as Joseph wrote on a clay **tablet**. "What a funny way to write," I thought.

They washed the tablet clean with water. While the tablet was wet they wrote on it. They wrote with a **stylus**.

The boys learned to write, but mostly they learned about God. Then Joseph and I helped his big brothers with their work.

While we worked with the men, the girls worked at home.

The women taught the girls to make coats. The girls also learned to make butter and bread.

WORSHIP

When all of the work was done, Joseph and I went back to our tent. "Will you tell me about one more thing, Joseph?"

"Yes. What is it you want to know?"

"Over there is a pile of rocks. It looks like something is burned on them."

Circle the best answer.

1.32　What do you think the burnt rocks were?

　　a.　a fireplace for cooking

　　b.　an altar to worship God

　　c.　a place to make smoke signals

• •

　　　"Those rocks are an **altar**. My father made the altar. It is where we pray to God."

　　　We know that sometimes we do things that God says are not right. God calls these bad things we do **sin**. Someone has to pay for that sin. One day God will send His Son to pay for that sin. Until then, we sacrifice animals to show that we believe in God. We kill and burn the animal here. God is happy to know we still love Him even though we sin against Him.

　　　"I watched Joseph and his family burn an animal on the altar. In this way they showed they believed in God. They worshiped Him. I thought about how I worshiped God."

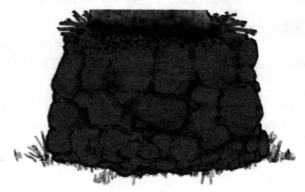

BIBLE

2 0 7

LIFEPAC TEST

20 / 25

Name _____

Date _____

Score _____

BIBLE 207: LIFEPAC TEST

Draw a line under words that are true about Joseph and his life.

1. had a dream
2. went to prison
3. did not go to a school
4. had a pretty coat
5. ate at a table

6. jumped in a well
7. rode on a camel
8. prayed to God
9. would sleep on a bed.
10. put food away for the people

Circle the word in each row that does not belong.

11.	camel	box	cow	oxen
12.	jar	butter	beans	bread
13.	mat	sleep	apple	night
14.	brother	sister	father	prison

Circle yes **or** no.

15. The people lived in a tent. yes no
16. The brothers loved Joseph. yes no

17.   They prayed by the altar.   yes   no

18.   Joseph was a slave in Egypt.   yes   no

19.   Joseph was happy to be in prison.   yes   no

Circle the correct word.

20.   We find the story of Joseph in _____.
       Leviticus   Mark   Genesis

21.   A _____ is when there is no food.
       feast   game   famine

22.   God gave Jesus to take sin out of His _____ in
       our life.
       sight   bright   night

23.   Joseph and his family worshiped God at an altar made
       of _____ .
       wood   bricks   rocks

24.   Joseph used an _____ lamp.
       oil   electric   orange

25.   God made a _____ thing out of a bad thing.
       good   black   brave

NOTES

Today we do not have to kill and burn animals to worship God. God wants us to love Him and to believe in His Son, Jesus. God gave Jesus to show us what God was like. God gave Jesus to die for our sin. We can tell Jesus we are sorry for our sin. Jesus will put all our sin out of God's sight. He will forgive us. Jesus is our friend and helps us not to sin. Jesus loves us. God wants us to ask Jesus to come into our life.

• •

 Talk about this Bible verse with a friend.

1.33 Learn John 3:16; with your teacher.

"For God so loved the world, that He gave His only begotten Son, that whosoever believeth in Him should not perish, but have everlasting life."

1.34 Say John 3:16 with your family.

Family check _____

Suddenly, I awoke. My Bible had fallen on the floor. I picked it up.

I looked at the picture of Joseph. He had on his coat of many colors.

I wanted to read the story of Joseph again.

Write the missing letters.

1.35   The pile of r ___ ___ ___ ___ was an altar.

1.36   Jesus takes away our s ___ ___ .

1.37   Joseph wrote on c ___ ___ ___ tablets.

1.38   God is our heavenly F ___ ___ ___ ___ ___ .

1.39   Joseph's f ___ ___ ___ ___ ___ would teach him.

1.40   Joseph worked with his b ___ ___ ___ ___ ___ ___ ___ .

1.41   The girls helped their m ___ ___ ___ ___ ___ ___ .

Teacher Check _____
                        Initial   Date

For this Self Test, study what you have read and done. The Self Test will check what you remember.

These words are jumbled (mujbled). **Can you spell them right? Put them in the right riddle.**

etnt   keydon   mpla

nmnaeBij   toac

1.01   I am Joseph's brother.
I am Joseph's little brother.
My name is _____ .

1.02   I can carry baskets.
People ride in my box.
I am a _____ .

1.03   I am made of goat hair.
I have two or three rooms.
I am a _____ .

1.04   They light me at night.
I burn oil.
I am a _____ .

1.05   I belong to Joseph.
I have many colors.
I am a _____ .

Draw lines to match these words to make sentences.

1.06   The boys wrote   at the altar.

1.07   Jacob told a   take away my sin.

1.08   They prayed to God   bread in the beans.

1.09   They dipped their   on clay tablets.

1.010   Jesus will   story about Noah.

Write the words in the blanks to finish John 3:16.

1.011   "For God so _____ the world that He

_____ His only begotten _____ ,

that whosoever believeth in _____ shall not

perish but have everlasting _____ .

 Teacher Check _____

Initial   Date

My Score

II. JOSEPH AS A MAN

When Joseph grew to be a man, God
helped him. God helped him to be **wise**
and good.

Joseph was made a **slave**. God helped
him to be a good slave. Joseph was
made a **ruler** after he was a slave.
God helped Joseph to be a good ruler.
When Joseph was a ruler, he helped
many people.

Joseph learned that God can make good things come out of bad things that other people do. This part of the LIFEPAC will show you how God helped Joseph when he was a man.

WORDS TO STUDY

bow		To bend your head or body in a very polite way.
famine	(fam ine)	A time when there is no food.
heavenly	(heav en ly)	
Father	(fa ther)	God.
prison	(pris on)	A place where people who break the law are locked up.
ruler	(ru ler)	Like a king.
secret	(se cret)	Something you do not tell anyone.
slave		A man or woman who is owned by someone else.
thin		One side is very close to the other side.
trader	(tra der)	Someone who buys and sells things.
wise		To know a lot about something.

Special Words

Egypt   Potiphar

Teacher Check _____

Initial   Date

SOLD BY HIS BROTHERS

Jacob had given Joseph a beautiful coat. The coat had many colors in it. Joseph's brothers were angry because they did not get a coat of colors. Joseph did what was right. The brothers did not like Joseph because he did what was right. They wanted what Joseph had. They were not kind to Joseph.

When Joseph was a young man, he had a strange dream. He saw the sun and the moon and eleven stars in the sky. In his dream the sun and the moon and the eleven stars all **bowed** down to him.

Joseph told his father about the dream. His brothers listened. They did not like what Joseph said.

"Are you saying that we will bow down to you?" they asked. They were very angry with Joseph.

One day Joseph's father called to him.

"Joseph, will you go and find your brothers, please. They are keeping the sheep. See how they are," Jacob said.

Joseph put on his beautiful coat and started out to find his brothers. He walked a long way. Soon he could see his brothers. He came closer to them.

When they saw him, they were angry. They saw his coat and were angry again.

One of them said, "Here comes that dreamer."

Another one said, "He has on that beautiful coat!"

They all said, "Let's get rid of him!"

Joseph was glad to find his brothers. But his brothers did not even smile at him. They grabbed him and pulled off his coat.

They put him down in an old well. Joseph was glad that the well had no water in it. It was dark down in the well, and Joseph was afraid.

Joseph thought, "Father will not know where I am." Then he thought, "God will take care of me." God made Joseph feel better. He was not afraid anymore. Joseph knew God was with him.

Study these words. When you see e, i, or y after the letter c, it has the /s/ sound.

1. The brother had a cross look on his fa<u>c</u>e.
2. Joseph did not live in a <u>c</u>ity.

2.1   Circle the words where the c says /s/.

calf	carrot	cat	city
climb	clock	come	corn
fence	ice	cane	pencil
princess	race	twice	voice

 Teacher Check _____

                         Initial   Date

The brothers sat down to eat their lunch. They didn't give Joseph anything to eat. They were thinking what to tell their father.

In a little while, some **traders** came by. When the brothers saw the traders, one brother said, "Why don't we sell Joseph? Joseph would make a good **slave**."

Joseph could hear his brothers talking. He thought, "What are they going to do with me?"

Joseph heard one brother say, "Would you like to buy a slave?"

The brothers took Joseph out of the well to show him to the traders. The traders said, "He is strong. He could work hard."

The traders gave Joseph's brothers some money. They put Joseph on a camel. Then the traders started on their way to Egypt with Joseph.

Joseph felt so sad. Joseph thought he would never see his father again. Then Joseph prayed. He knew his **heavenly Father** would take care of Him.

 **Learn this verse.**

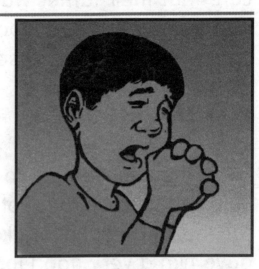

2.2 Say Psalm 56:3 to a friend.
"What time I am afraid,
I will trust in thee [God]."

 Teacher Check _____
      Initial   Date

 **Number the sentences** 1, 2, 3, 4 **to show when each thing happened.**

2.3 _____ Joseph was put in the well.

2.4 _____ Joseph found his brothers.

2.5 _____ Joseph was sold to traders.

2.6 _____ Joseph had a dream.

Joseph was taken to Egypt as a slave. His brothers went back home. They took Joseph's beautiful coat back to their father, Jacob.

The brothers showed the coat to Jacob. Jacob thought Joseph had been killed by an animal. Jacob was very sad and cried for many days. Jacob loved his son Joseph. The brothers did not care that their father was sad. The brothers did not care about Joseph. They were glad that Joseph was gone.

PUT IN PRISON

When Joseph got to Egypt, the men sold him to Potiphar. Potiphar worked for the king. Potiphar liked Joseph. He gave him a very good job. God helped Joseph to do his work well.

Potiphar's wife was not a good woman. She wanted Joseph to do a very bad thing. Joseph would not do it. Potiphar's wife was very angry and told a lie about Joseph. Potiphar listened to his wife and put Joseph in **prison**.

Poor Joseph was sad again. He was put in prison. He had not done anything wrong. Joseph prayed to God. He knew his heavenly Father was with him even in prison.

Joseph was in prison a long time. He made some friends there. Some of them had worked for the king. One day one of his friends was told to go back to the palace. Joseph's friend would work for the king again.

Write the numbered letters to match the numbers in the last sentence. Put the letters in the blank. Read the sentence.

Joseph thought —

    Why were my brothers angry with me?

    Why did my brothers sel**l** me?
                          2

    Why **a**m I in **p**riso**n**?
      3   1   4

This sentence tells you why.

2.7   God had a beautiful ____ ____ ____ ____ for Joseph.
                                 1   2   3   4

One night the king had a dream. In the dream the king saw seven fat cows. The fat cows were eating grass by the river. Then a funny thing happened. Seven **thin** cows came and ate the seven fat cows. Do cows eat cows? They did in the king's dream.

The king knew that cow's didn't eat cows. He called his **wise** men to help him.

"Can you tell me why the thin cows ate the fat cows in my dream?" asked the king.

The wise men looked at each other. "We do not know why the thin cows ate the fat cows. We do not know what this dream is about," said one of the wise men.

The king was not happy. Then the friend remembered Joseph from the prison. Joseph's friend went to the king. "I know a man in prison who can help you" he said. "His name is Joseph."

"Go to the prison quickly," said the king. "Ask Joseph to help me."

Joseph came quickly when they called him for the king.

Joseph was excited because he was leaving the prison. "What does the king want?" he thought.

Joseph stood before the king. The king told Joseph about his dream where the thin cows were eating the fat cows.

"Do you know what my dream means?" the king asked.

Study these words. When the letters ea are in a word, usually the first vowel is long (says its name) and the second vowel is silent. For example, the ea in ice cream says the sound of long e /ē/.

Write the best word in the sentence.

2.8   Joseph had a _____ .

bean   dream   seam

2.9   Jacob made a box _____ for the donkey.

seat   beak   speak

2.10   The family ate _____ with their fingers.

peak   meat   leaf

2.11   "What does my dream _____ ?" asked the king.

mean   steam   beam

2.12   The women cooked _____ over the fire.

beans   dreams   seams

"God showed me what the dream means," answered Joseph.

"God said that the seven fat cows mean that a lot of food will grow for seven years. The seven thin cows mean that no food will grow for seven years. We will have a **famine**. We must save food for seven years while food is

page 33 (thirty-three)

growing well. We will save food to eat when things will not grow," Joseph said.

PICKED FOR A RULER

Then the king said, "Joseph, you are very smart. I will make you a **ruler**. You take care of the food. Save some food so that we will not be hungry in the seven years with no food." The king did not know that God was helping Joseph.

Joseph thought, "God is good to me."

Joseph worked hard. He made the people put a lot of food away. In seven years the famine began. The people in Egypt had enough food because they had saved it. People in other countries had no food. They were hungry.

Write the word from the box on the line. You will use one word two times.

famine	God	saved
food	ruler	seven

2.13   The fat cows mean a lot of food for _____ years.

2.14   The thin cows mean no food will grow for _____ years.

2.15   No food means a _____ .

2.16   The king made Joseph a _____ .

page 34 (thirty-four)

2.17   Joseph will take care of the _____ .

2.18   Joseph said, " _____ is good to me."

2.19   The people in Egypt had enough food because they _____ it.

HELPED IN A FAMINE

Joseph's father and his brothers did not have food and were hungry. Jacob, their father, called the brothers to him and said, "Will you go to Egypt and buy some food?"

So the brothers got ready to go. They rode a long way on their donkeys. Then the brothers came to Egypt. They went to the king's house. The brothers asked if they could buy food.

Joseph said, "Yes, you may buy food." Joseph was surprised. These men were his brothers. Joseph knew his brothers, but his brothers did not know him. The brothers bowed down to Joseph. The dream Joseph had years ago was true. Joseph's brothers did bow down to him.

Joseph's brothers returned home, but ran out of food again. They returned to Egypt to buy more food.

This time Joseph could not keep his **secret**. He hugged them and said, "I am Joseph, your brother." The brothers were surprised. They were sorry about what they had done to Joseph.

The brothers remembered the dream Joseph had many years ago. They did bow down to him now. They knew that God was with Joseph.

Joseph said, "Go back home and get Jacob, our father. Bring Benjamin and your families. Live here with me. I will take care of you. You did something bad, but God sent me here so that you would have food."

Draw lines to match.

2.20   Joseph's brothers came   his brothers.

2.21   Joseph was surprised to see   for food.

2.22   The brothers bowed down   of his family.

2.23   Joseph said, "I am   to Joseph.

2.24   Joseph took care   your brother."

Learn this verse.

2.25   Say Romans 8:28 to a helper.
"And we know that all things work together for good to them that love God."

Teacher Check _____
                Initial   Date

Optional activity.

2.26   Read the story of Joseph in Genesis 37-46 from the Bible with your family. Then talk about Joseph and his family.

Teacher Check _____
                       Initial   Date

Study what you have read and done for this last Self Test. This Self Test will check what you remember in your studies of all parts in this LIFEPAC. The last Self Test will tell you what parts of the LIFEPAC you need to study again.

SELF TEST 2

Write the word from the box on the line.

altar	Joseph
famine	The brothers
Jacob	

2.01   _____ taught Joseph to write.

2.02   _____ had a coat of many colors.

2.03   _____ bowed down to Joseph.

2.04   When no food would grow, they had a

       _____ .

2.05   Joseph's family prayed to God at the _____ .

Draw lines to match the words that belong together.

2.06	The king dreamed	is God.
2.07	Our heavenly Father	his brothers.
2.08	A famine means	Joseph's brother.
2.09	Joseph knew	about seven fat cows.
2.010	Benjamin was	there is no food.

Who said it? Put the right word before the sentence.

You may use a word from this list more than one time.

brothers   Jacob   Joseph

king   wise men

2.011 _____ "We will not bow down to you, Joseph."

2.012 _____ "My home is a tent. I live with my brother, Benjamin

2.013 _____ "Joseph, will you go and find your brothers? They are with the sheep."

2.014 _____ "God will take care of me. I am not afraid."

2.015 _____ "Ask Joseph to help me with my dream. I want to know about the fat and thin cows."

2.016 _____ "We do not know what this dream is about. Cows don't eat cows."

2.017 _____ "God showed me what the dream meant. I could help the king."

2.018 _____ "Joseph is my son."

2.019 _____ "God sent me here so that you would have food. Come live with me."

2.020 _____ "Save some food so that we will not be hungry."

  Teacher Check _____

16 / 20

Initial   Date

My Score

Before taking the LIFEPAC Test, you should do these self checks.

1. Did you do good work on your last Self Test?

2. Did you study again those parts of the LIFEPAC you did not remember?

   Check one: ☐ Yes (good)
                ☐ No (ask your teacher)

3. Do you know all the new words in "Words to Study"?

   Check one: ☐ Yes (good)
                ☐ No (ask your teacher)

NOTES

NOTES